Recorder Wizard

Follow the **magical** comic strip adventures of Johnny and Sophie as the **Recorder Wizard** teaches you **how to play!**

By Emma Coulthard

Contents

Published by
Chester Music
8/9 Frith Street, London W1D 3JB, England.

Exclusive Distributors:
Music Sales Limited
Distribution Centre,
Newmarket Road,
Bury St Edmunds,
Suffolk IP33 3YB, England.
Music Sales Corporation
257 Park Avenue South,
New York, NY10010,
United States of America.
Music Sales Pty Limited
120 Rothschild Avenue,
Rosebery, NSW 2018,
Australia.

Order No. CH68574
ISBN 1-84449-564-7
This book © Copyright 2004 by Chester Music.

Unauthorised reproduction of any part of this publication by any means including photocopying is an infringement of copyright.

Written by Emma Coulthard
Project editor Heather Ramage
Illustrated by Bob Bond
Comic strip plot by Ed Chatelier
Art agency The Edge Group
Design and layout Chloë Alexander Design
Music setting Michael McCartney

CD recorded, mixed and mastered by Jonas Persson
Music arranged by Rick Cardinali
Recorder Emma Coulthard
Voice-over artist Mike Winsor

Your Guarantee of Quality
As publishers, we strive to produce every book to the highest commercial standards.
　As publishers, we strive to produce every book to the highest commercial standards.
　The music has been freshly engraved and the book has been carefully designed to minimise awkward page turns and to make playing from it a real pleasure.
　Particular care has been given to specifying acid-free, neutral-sized paper made from pulps which have not been elemental chlorine bleached. This pulp is from farmed sustainable forests and was produced with special regard for the environment.
　Throughout, the printing and binding have been planned to ensure a sturdy, attractive publication which should give years of enjoyment.
　If your copy fails to meet our high standards, please inform us and we will gladly replace it.

www.recorderwizard.co.uk

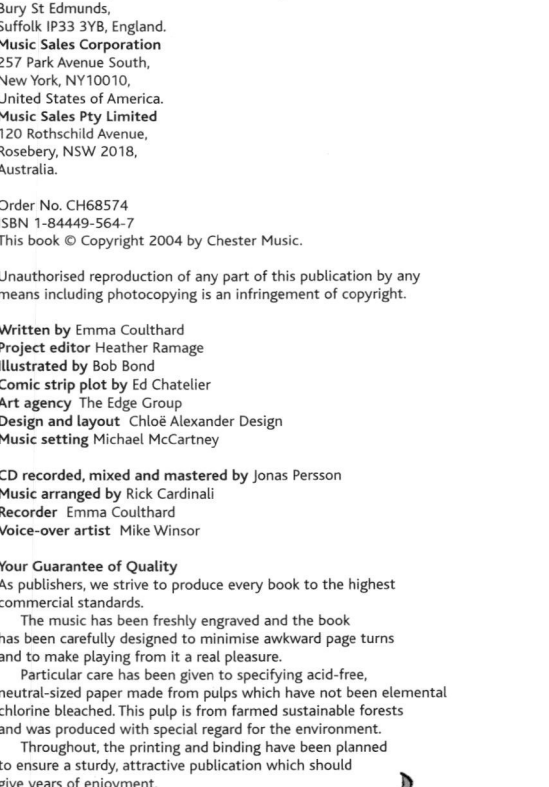

The Magic Recorder

Mouthpiece

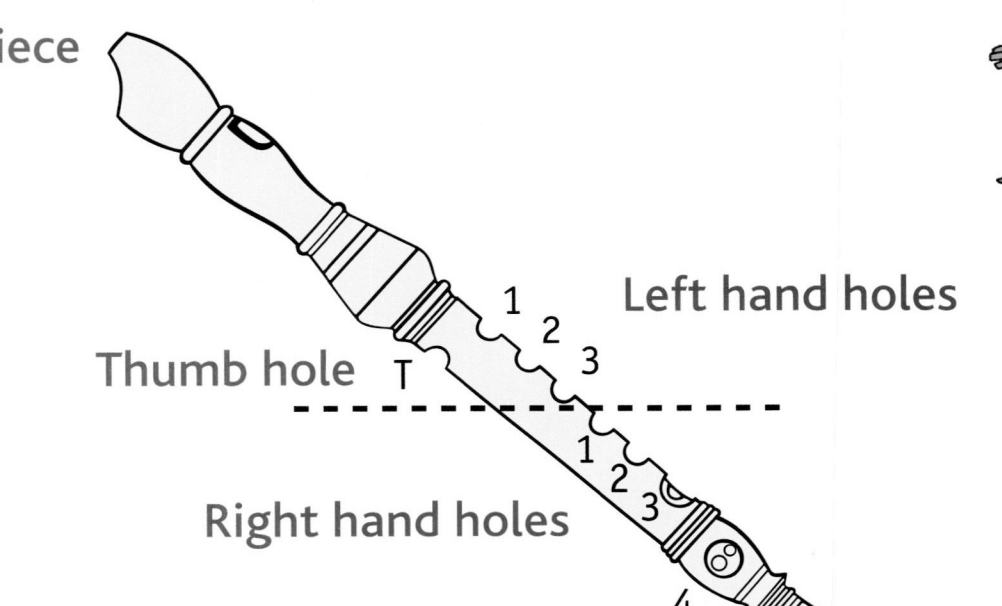

Left hand holes

Thumb hole

Right hand holes

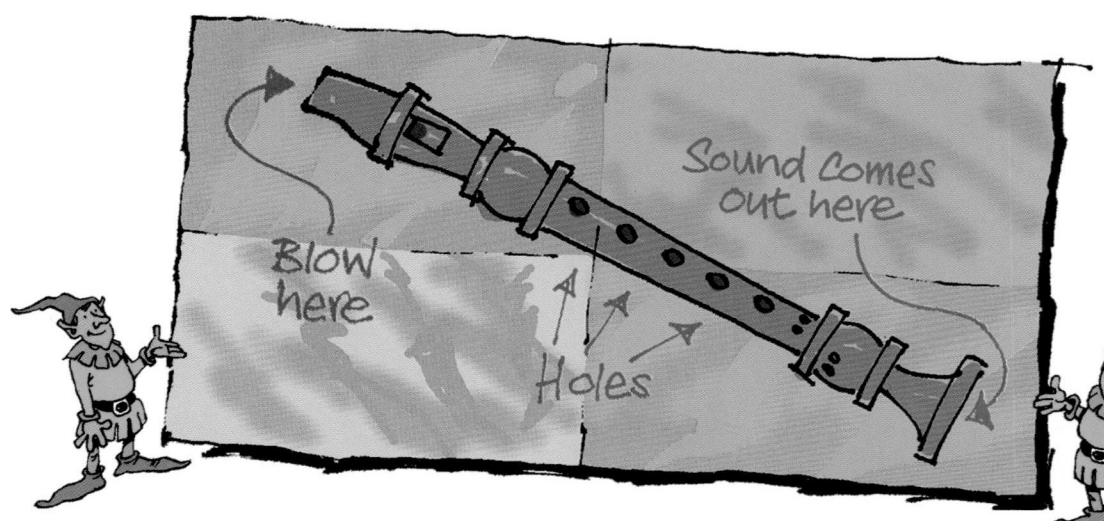

The Three Skills

1 The Breath of a Soft Breeze

Breathe deeply and
blow gently at your hand.

Feel the cool air
on your fingers.

2 The Power of Speech

You must speak into the recorder
to make a nice, clear sound.

DOO...DOO...
DOO...DOO...

Practise saying
doo, doo, doo, doo...

Place your fingers on the holes.

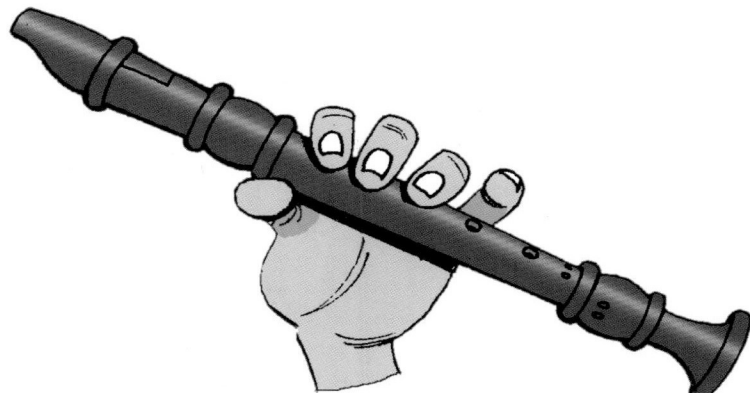

First your left hand
with your thumb on the back hole.

Now move them on and off
the holes as if they
are dancing.

Then your right.

7

FIRSTLY, THE BREATH OF A SOFT BREEZE...

THEN, THE POWER OF SPEECH, YOU SHOULD BE GOOD AT THAT, AS YOU NEVER STOP TALKING...

THIRDLY, THE MOVEMENT OF DANCING FINGERS...

B Is For Broomstick

This is how you play B

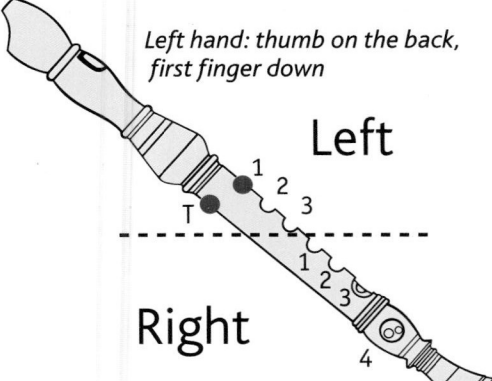

Left hand: thumb on the back, first finger down

Left

Right

Try some long Bs:

B ——— B ———

B ——— B ———

And some short ones:

B — B — B — B —

Remember to blow gently, and to say *doo*!

How many things beginning with 'B' can you find in the comic strip above?

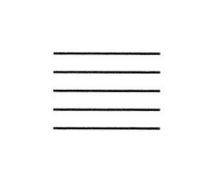

This is the stave.

This is called a treble clef. It sits at the beginning of each stave.

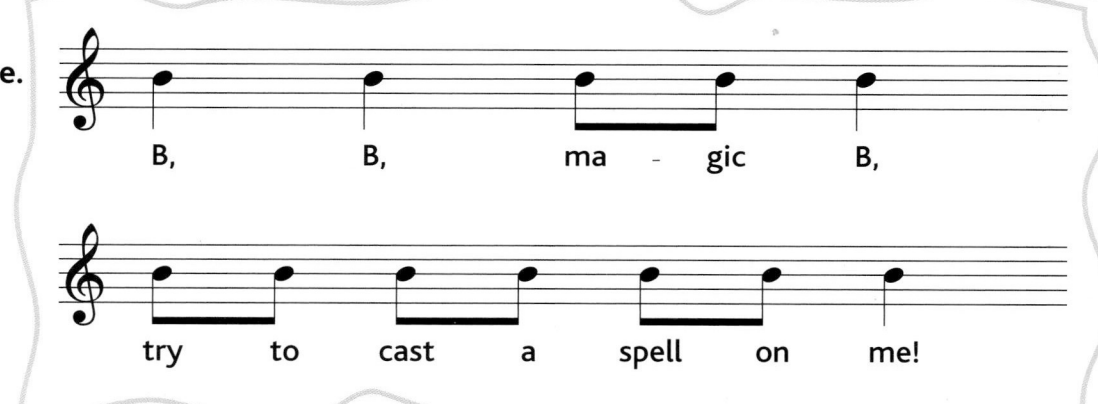

B, B, ma - gic B, try to cast a spell on me!

9

The stave has five lines and four spaces, and B is written on the middle line.

A Is For Apple

Here is A

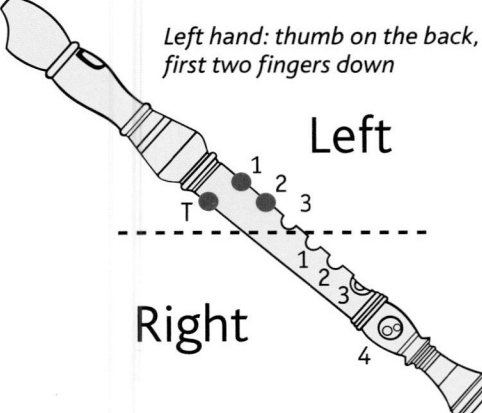

Left hand: thumb on the back, first two fingers down

Left

Right

Try some long ones:

A ——— A ———

A ——— A ———

And some short ones:

A— A— A— A—

Say *doo* with your tongue and speak each note clearly.

NOW SOPHIE SAYS IT'S **BORING**... SHE CALLS ME JOHNNY-ONE-NOTE...

SO...LET'S LEARN THE **NEXT** ONE.

MIDDLE FINGER DOWN ALSO — THAT'S AN **A**...

COOL!

How many things beginning with 'A' can you find in the comic strip above?

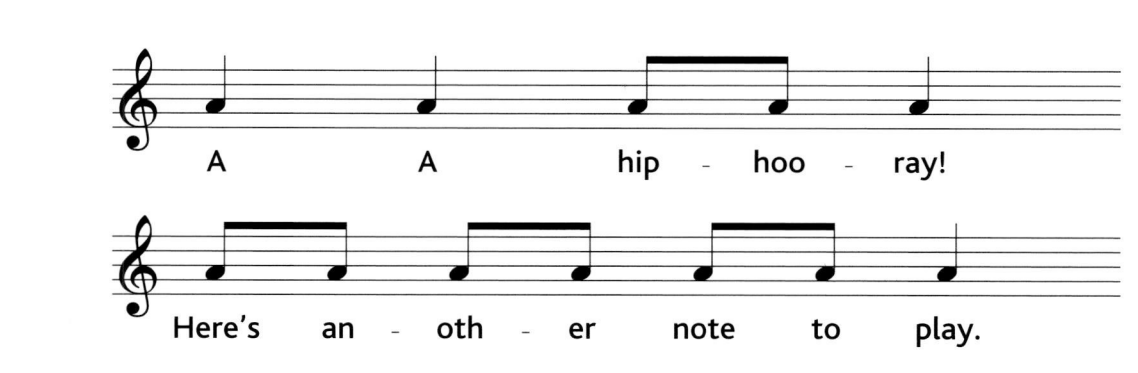

A   A   hip – hoo – ray!

Here's   an – oth – er   note   to   play.

11

A is written on the second space up.

LISTEN, SOPHIE—I HAVE ANOTHER SOUND...

SO, WHAT HAPPENS IF YOU PUT **BOTH** NOTES TOGETHER?

Dance With Me

Tracks
6-7

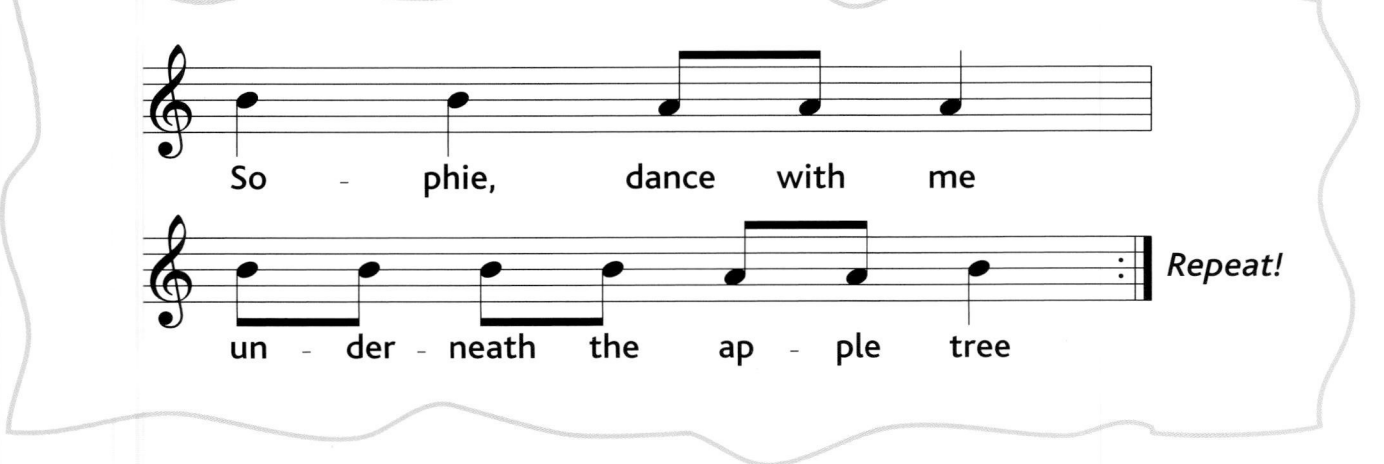

So - phie, dance with me

Repeat!

un - der - neath the ap - ple tree

12

Some elves walk:

1   **2**   **3**   **4**

13

Little twins run:

1   and   **2**   and   **3**   and   **4**   and

Together,
they make patterns:

Spell   Ma - gic   Spell   Spell

Copy Cat

Track 8

Can you clap these patterns after you hear them?

14

Mary Had A Little Lamb

Tracks
13-14

This piece has four beats in a bar.
Play slowly, one beat at a time, until you are ready to put it all together.

18

Ma - ry had a lit - tle lamb, lit - tle lamb, lit - tle lamb,

Baa!

Ma - ry had a lit - tle lamb, its fleece was white as snow.

HEY! THAT WAS THREE BLIND MICE...

NOW TRY THIS ONE!

WHAT ARE ALL THESE SHEEP DOING IN THE BEDROOM?

HA HA! MARY HAD A LITTLE LAMB!

THEY'RE STILL COMING! THIS ROOM ISN'T BIG ENOUGH...

TIME TO **BRANCH** OUT THEN... ALIKAZAM!

Three Blind Mice

The vertical lines are called barlines.

They divide the notes into groups of equal length, called bars.

The number at the beginning of the music tells you how many beats are in each bar.

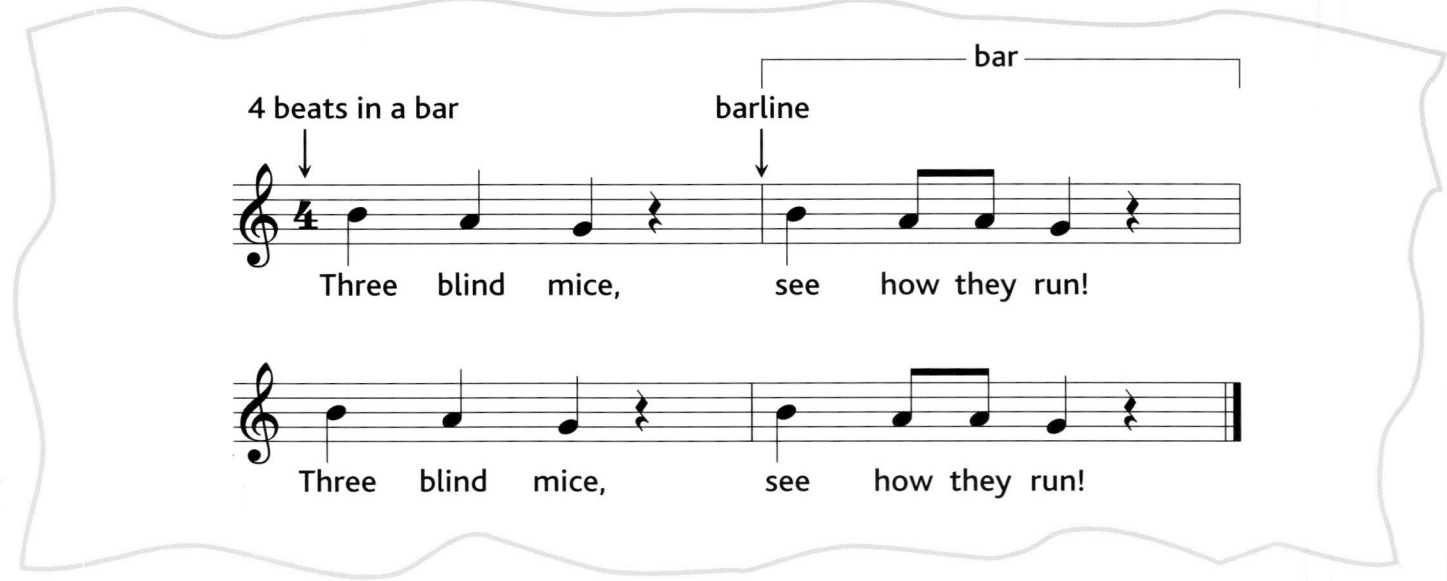

4 beats in a bar

bar

barline

Three   blind   mice,   see   how they run!

Three   blind   mice,   see   how they run!

17

= 1 beat

= 1 beat

Have A Rest

When an elf needs to rest, he has a little sleep.

When we want silence in music, we have a little rest:

There are long rests and short rests.

This one lasts for just one beat – so don't fall asleep!

16

This is G

Left hand: thumb on the back, three fingers down

Left

Right

G,   G,   Ghost ...   ooooh!

G,   G,   Ghost ...   ooooh!

G is written on the second line up.

Speak each note gently.

15

How many things beginning with 'G' can you find in the comic strip above?

Copy Cat

Listen and Play!

B A B

B B A

B A G

G A G

? ? ?

What are the mystery notes? Answers at the back of the book!

Striding

Apart from walking and running,
some elves like to take big strides.

In music, it looks like this:

The stride takes up two beats.

1 2 (two beats)

E Is For Enchanted

Tracks 16-17

This is E

Left hand: thumb on the back, three fingers down

Left

Right

Right hand: first two fingers down

20

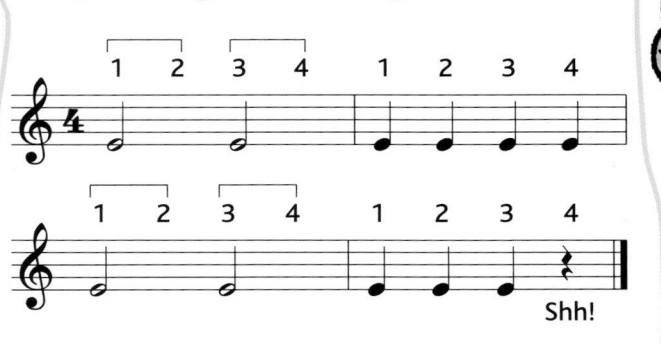

E is written on the bottom line.

Speak in a whisper!

Enchanted E

3 beats in a bar

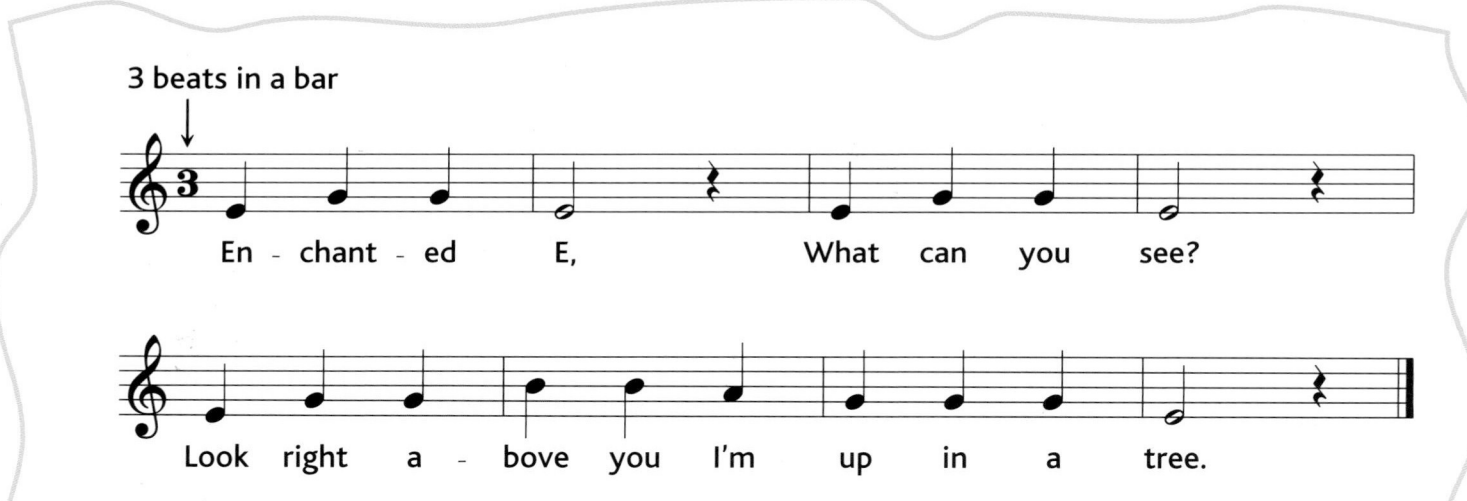

En - chant - ed E, What can you see?

Look right a - bove you I'm up in a tree.

21

Forest Sounds

You can make amazing sound effects on the recorder.

Owls

22

E is good for owls.

Too - whit,   too - woo!

Cuckoos

B and G sounds like a cuckoo. The dot on the note tells you to make the sound really short. It's called a 'staccato'. Say *tut* with your tongue, instead of *doo*.

Cuc - koo!   Cuc - koo!

Yellow Bird

This ⌣ or ⌢ is a slur. It tells you to join the notes together without tonguing in between.

Just speak the first note and move your fingers for the others in the slur.

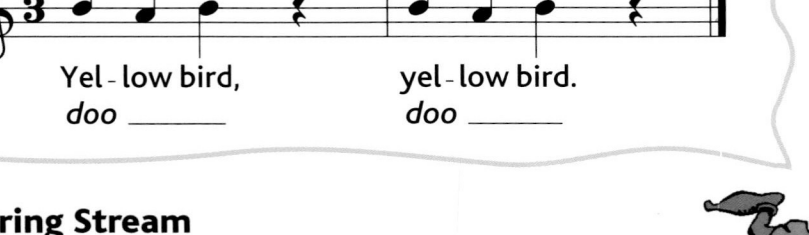

Yel - low bird,   yel - low bird.
doo _____   *doo* _____

Murmuring Stream

Slurring repeated notes together makes a lovely murmuring sound.

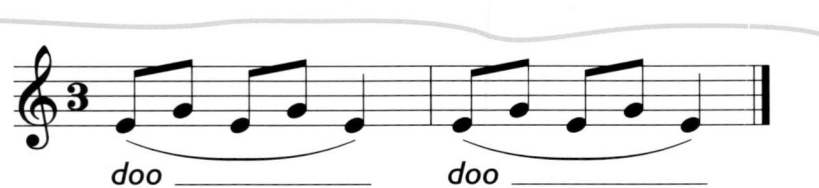

doo _____   *doo* _____

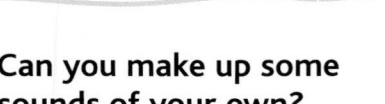

Can you make up some sounds of your own?

Cuckoo! ... *murmuring stream* ...

... *yellow bird* ... ... *owl* ...

23

Song Of The Elves

24

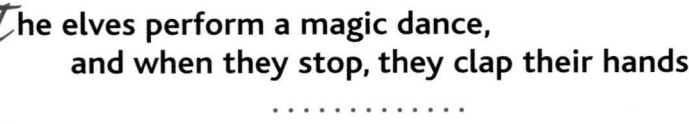

*T*he elves perform a magic dance,
　　and when they stop, they clap their hands.

. . . .

*T*hey leap about and shout and scream,
　　with lots of clapping in between.

. . . .

*T*he order of the cards is clear,
　　but which is which? Just use your ear!

. . . .

*A*nd if you are in any doubt,
　　you're going to have to work it out!

. . . .

Rhythm Puzzle

Clapping is a hoot!

These are the clapping rhythms from the song,
but they are in the wrong order.

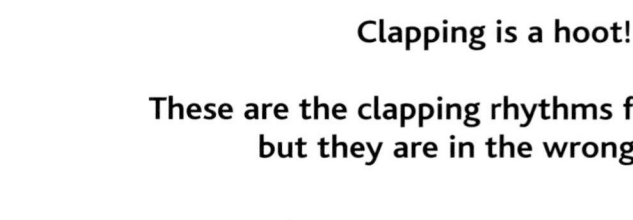

Can you work out which is which
by listening to the song,
and then write them in the boxes?

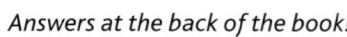

Answers at the back of the book!

Very gently

27

How many things beginning with 'D' can you find in the picture above?

The Dragon's Lair

28

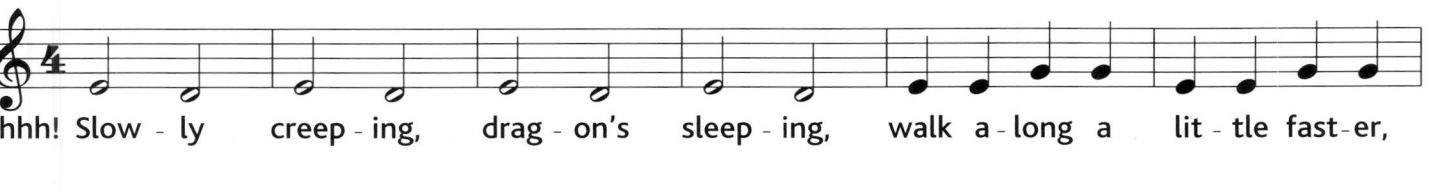

Shhh! Slow - ly creep - ing, drag - on's sleep - ing, walk a - long a lit - tle fast - er,

may - be you can just get past her, run, run, run, the deed is done the drag - on is a - wake!

Under Attack!

Quickly

29

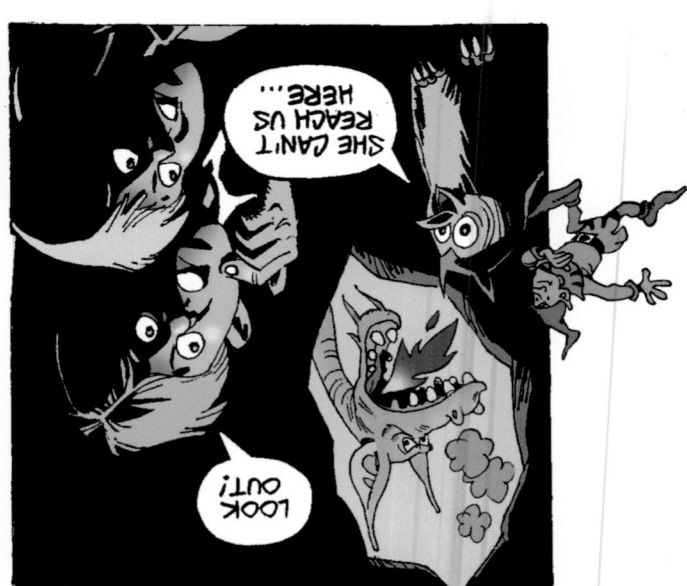

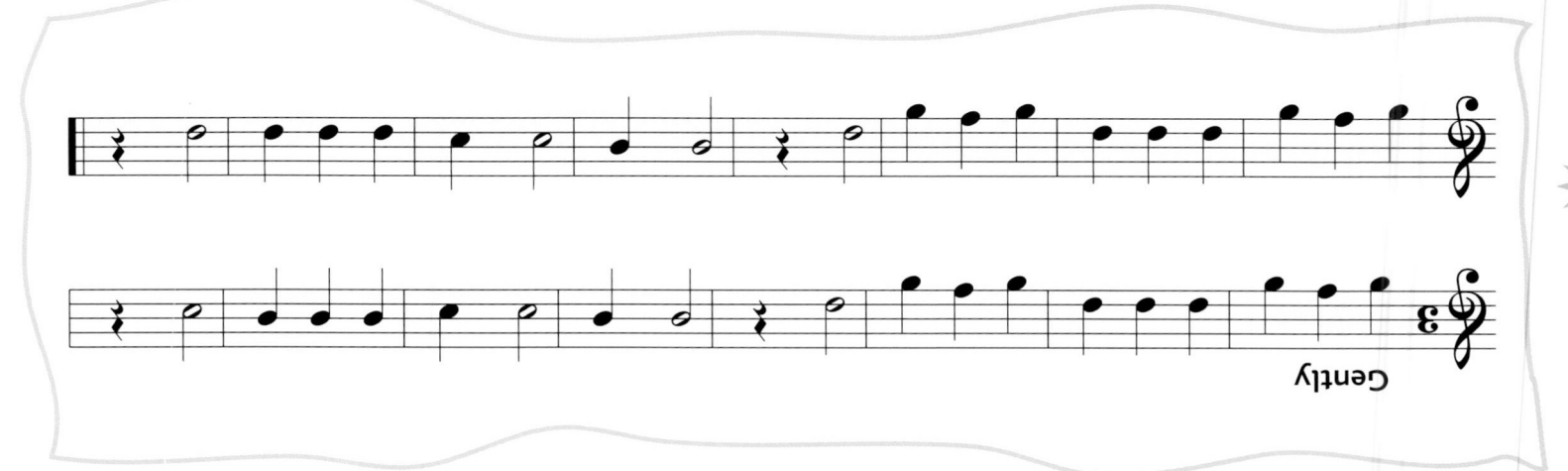

Gently

Lullaby Tracks **32-33**

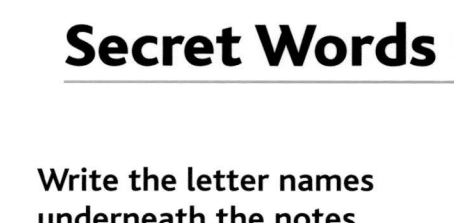

Secret Words Puzzle

Can you work out what the secret words are?

Write the letter names underneath the notes.

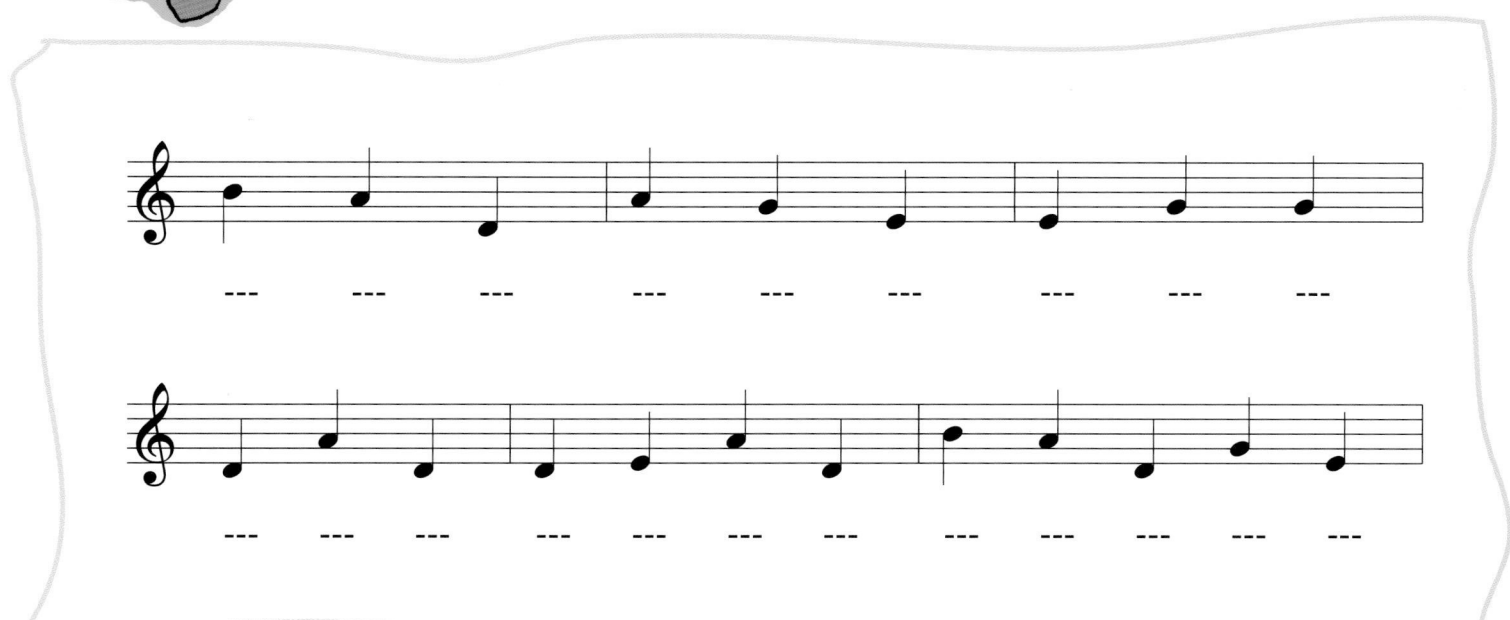

Answers at the back of the book!

32

Welcome to my home!

Write down each note letter to find out the password - then speak for access.

Oh, and please wipe your feet!

Thank you,

Wizard

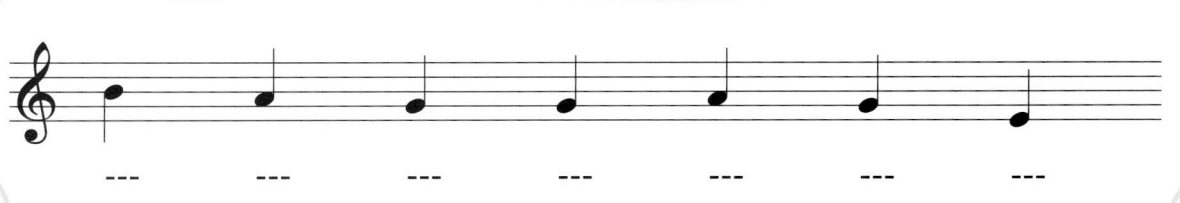

Answer at the back of the book!

33

Clock Chimes

This note: 𝅗𝅥. lasts for three beats.

You'll need plenty of air!

Trumpet Fanfare

Brightly

35

Celebrate!

36

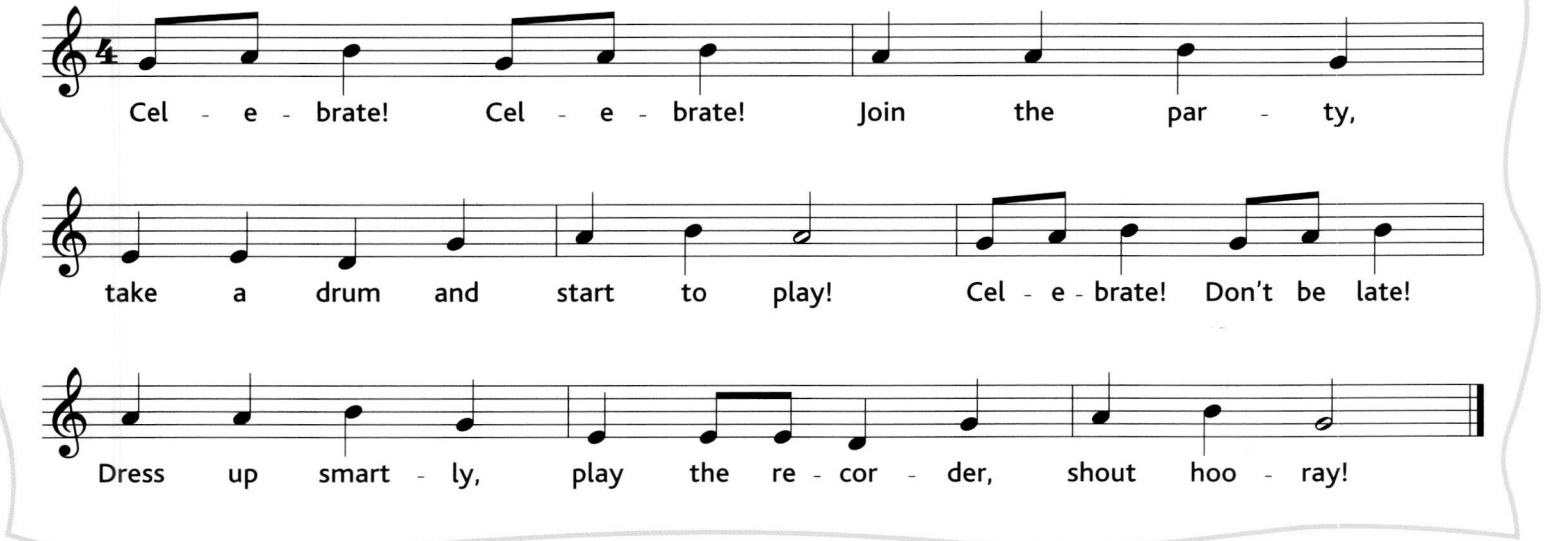

Cel - e - brate! Cel - e - brate! Join the par - ty,

take a drum and start to play! Cel - e - brate! Don't be late!

Dress up smart - ly, play the re - cor - der, shout hoo - ray!

Dancing Elves

Lively

Danc – ing elves, Danc – ing elves, they know how to please them–selves.

Danc – ing elves, Danc – ing elves, when they are to – ge – ther.

Round and round in rings they go, jump – ing high and stoop – ing low.

Danc – ing elves, Danc – ing elves, they have fun what – e – ver!

37

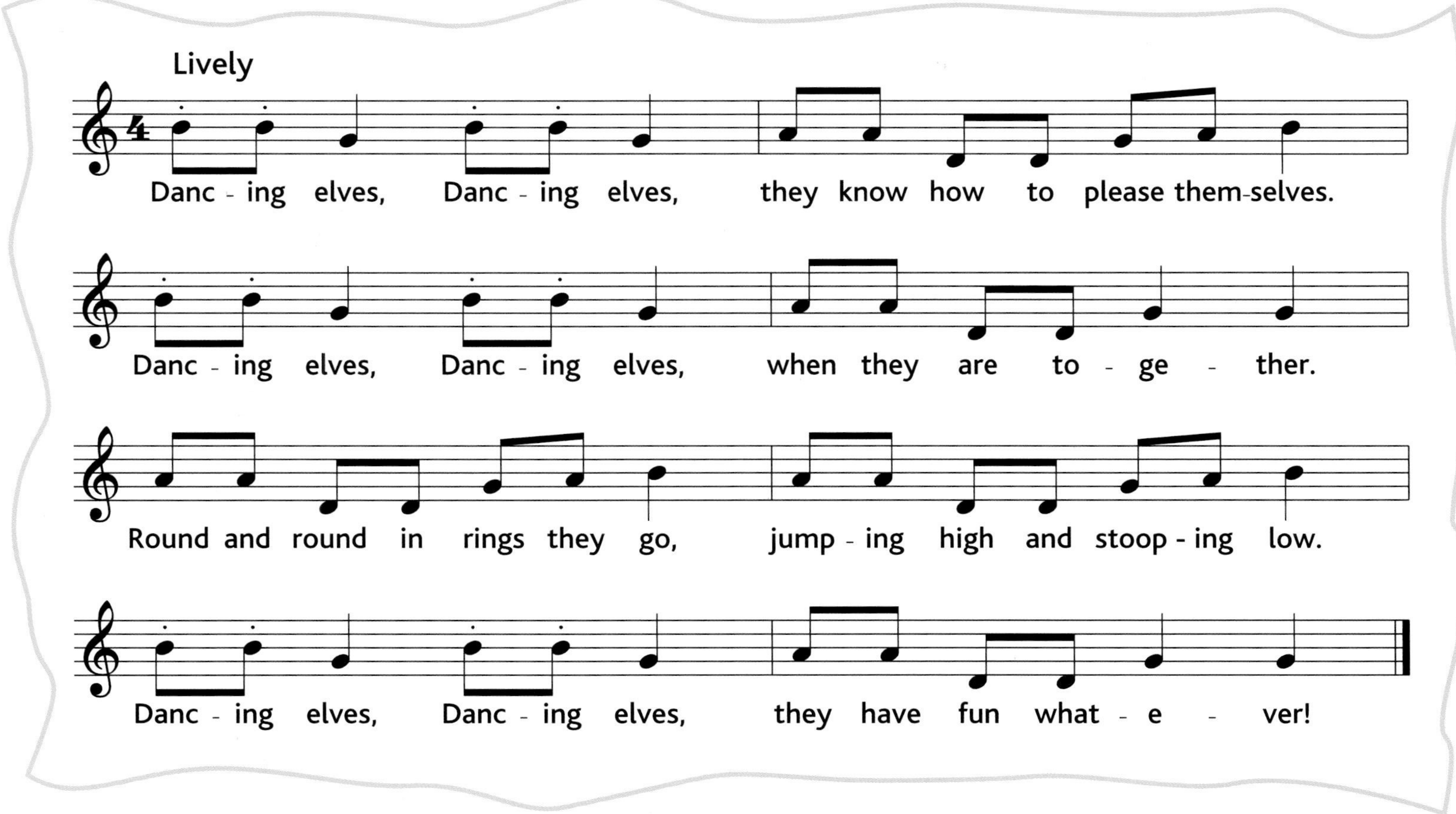

Uncle Angus

Un - cle An - gus hav - ing fun, B B A A G. A -

-way down in the Am - a - zon, B B A A

G. With a jun - gle here and a jun - gle there,

here a squeak! there a squeak! Ev' - ry - where a hee! hee!

Un - cle An - gus hav - ing fun, B B A A G.

39

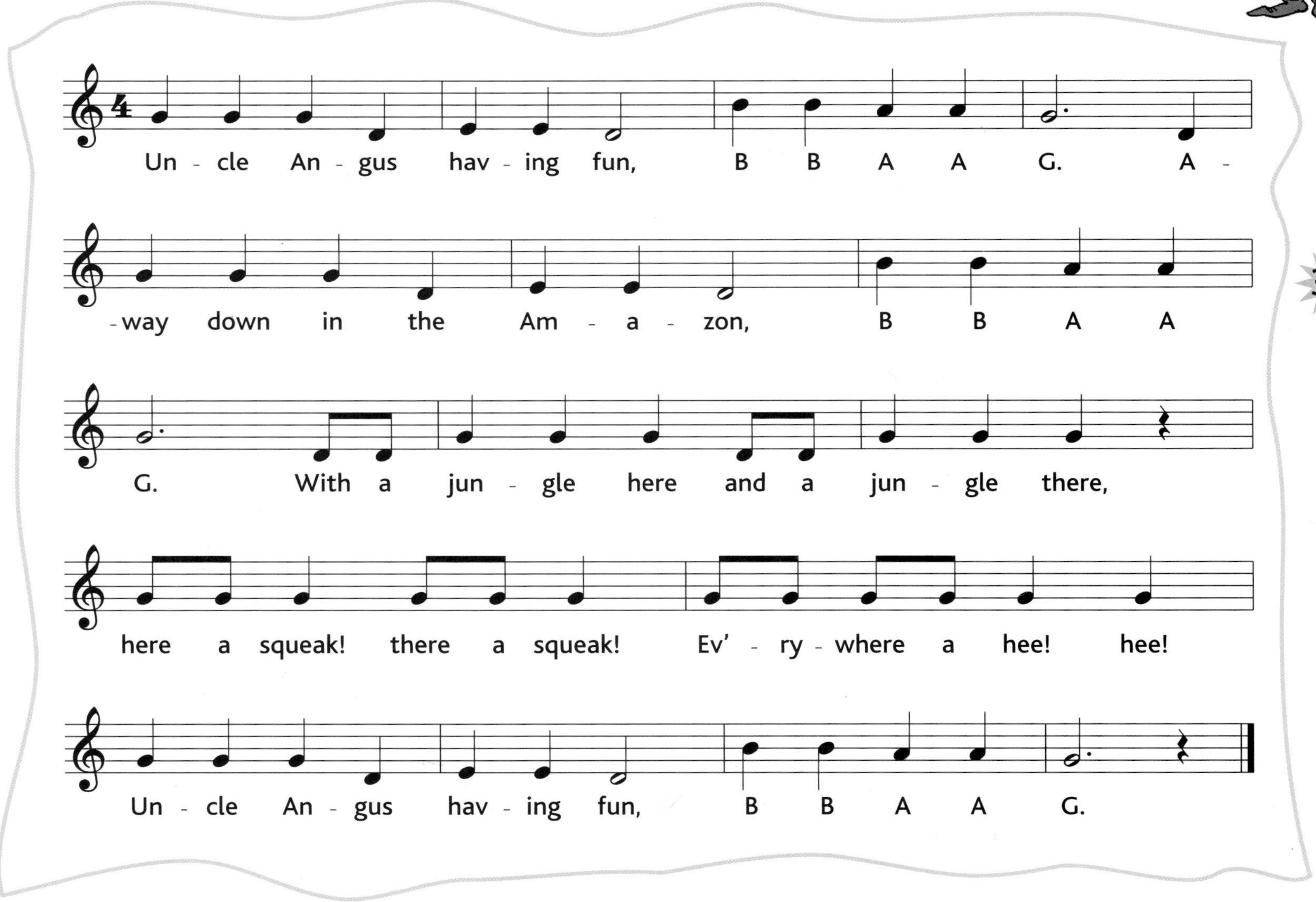

Answers To Puzzles

Copy Cat page 19
G, A, B

Rhythm Puzzle page 25
The rhythms from the song are clapped in this order:

40

Secret Words page 31
The secret words are: BAD, AGE, EGG, DAD, DEAD, BADGE

Welcome To My Home Puzzle page 33
The password is: BAGGAGE

CD Track Listing

Page numbers in brackets.
Each tune has two tracks – the first is a
model recorder version; the second is the
backing track only.

Printed in Singapore